Engraving by Edward Seager which appeared on Academy diplomas during the nineteenth century

Everybody Works But John Paul Jones

A PORTRAIT OF THE U.S. NAVAL ACADEMY, 1845–1915

By Mame Warren and Marion E. Warren

Everybody works but John Paul Jones!
  He lies around all day,
Body pickled in alcohol
  On a permanent jag, they say.
Middies stand around him
  Doing honor to his bones;
Everybody works in "Crabtown"
  But John Paul Jones!

NAVAL INSTITUTE PRESS
Annapolis, Maryland

By the same authors

The Train's Done Been and Gone: An Annapolis Portrait, 1859–1910

Library of Congress Cataloging in Publication Data
Warren, Mame, 1950–
    Everybody works but John Paul Jones.
    1. United States Naval Academy—History—19th
century. 2. United States Naval Academy—History—
20th century. I. Warren, Marion E. II. Title.
V415.L1W37   359'.007'1173   81–38373
ISBN 0–87021–734–8   AACR2

Printed in the United States of America

Acknowledgments

Discovering the multitude of images from which this collection was culled was a delightsome surprise. The original notion of exploring vintage photographs of the Naval Academy arose in discussions with David Raine, Jr. Our intention was to publish a revised edition of *The Train's Done Been and Gone,* our very popular portrait of Annapolis between 1859 and 1910. This time, however, we decided we would include a selection of period photographs of the Academy.

The wealth of material we found at once suggested that there were more than enough photographs readily available for a separate, companion volume to *The Train.* We took our idea to Captains William S. Busik and Roy C. Smith III at the U.S. Naval Academy Alumni Association: their response was enthusiastic and we left with a large print of John Paul Jones's second (or was it third?) funeral. The next logical step was a meeting with Richard R. Hobbs at the Naval Institute Press. The result is this book.

Along the way, many people were of considerable help to us, generously sharing their time and knowledge as well as illustrations. We found many sources within the walls of the Academy. Time and again Alice S. Creighton, Pamela J. Sherbert, and Mary Rose Catalfamo of Special Collections at Nimitz Library, and across the hall in Archives, Jane H. Price delved into their holdings, revealing a treasure trove seemingly without end. Patty M. Maddocks, director of the Naval Institute's Library and Photographic Services, shared, among other things, a fine collection of early stereographs. Curator James W. Cheevers kindly opened to our camera case after case at the Naval Academy Museum. Edward P. Wilson, Jr., Naval Academy Publications Officer, and Thomas F. Bates, Sports Information Director, Naval Academy Athletic Association, also permitted us to probe their files.

We were similarly welcomed by Charles S. Haberlein of the Naval History Division at the Washington Navy Yard and Leroy Bellamy at the Library of Congress. Each has an impressive command of his huge collection of photographs.

As always, Phebe Jacobsen made research at the Maryland Hall of Records a pleasure; we particularly prize the entries concerning the very early history of the Academy among the *Annapolis Corporation Proceedings* which she shared with us. We are also grateful to Sue Collins for providing us with microfilms of early issues of the *Evening Capital.*

Identifying and dating materials was often a pleasurable task for then our good friend Professor Emeritus Neville T. Kirk would come and pore over the photographs with us by the hour. And of course our work was made immeasurably easier for having Jack Sweetman's *The U.S. Naval Academy: An Illustrated History* (Naval Institute Press, 1979) as our textbook, his extensive bibliography being most useful in suggesting sources.

The intimate impression of life as a naval cadet or midshipman conveyed on these pages is due in large part to the generosity of private individuals who shared family pictures with us. We wish to thank Margaret Weems, Margaret F. Van Gilder, Lula Furlong, Andrew McIntyre, Captain Roy Smith III, Rear Admiral Hubert Strange, W. T. Cluverius, Anne Ansel, Emmy Marshall, Azalea Leckszas, Sally Court Brown, and Rear Admiral W. F. Fitzgerald, Jr.

Once again we are indebted to Calvert Chapline for his personal attention to this project from its inception, and to Gordon Chapline and all the good folks at Wolk Press for their meticulous work in obtaining such superior reproductions. We are grateful also for guidance in design, both past and present, from Gerard A. Valerio and Beverly S. Baum, and for excellent editorial sleuthing by Mary Veronica Amoss. A special thank you is due to Frank Parsons whose understanding and technical support has been a continual blessing.

Preeminent among the photographers whose work is contained in this volume is Frances Benjamin Johnston, who was commissioned by the U.S. Government to portray the Academy and its students for the Columbian Exposition in Chicago in 1893. Photographers Henry Schaefer, Charles H. Hopkins, William Chase, David Bachrach, F. M. Zuller, E. H. Pickering, and Lynn McAboy are also represented, with much appreciation for their artistry. We were fortunate as well to have available the originals of drawings by Edward Seager and Park Benjamin.

Finally, and most warmly, we acknowledge the constant and inspirational support we received from our friends and family, especially our mother and wife, Mary G. Warren, our comrades Flora P. Chambers and Sally Mann, advisors Barbara Vandegrift and Bob Davenport, and a people and a place called Stoneyfoot.

Whereas the President of the United States in his late message to Congress has recommended to that body to make provision by Law, for the establishment of a Naval School, and whereas it is believed that the City of Annapolis possesses many and great advantages for the location of such an Institution, which if properly understood and duly appreciated might secure to it an object so beneficial to its interests. Therefore

RESOLVED by the Mayor, Recorder, Aldermen and Common Council of the City of Annapolis that the representative in the Congress from the Second Congressional District of Maryland be respectfully requested to introduce a Resolution in the House of Representatives of the United States to appoint a committee to inquire into the expediency of establishing a Naval School in the City of Annapolis or to bring the subject before Congress in any other manner that may seem most expedient. Resolved that the Senators of Maryland in Congress be respectfully requested to use their influence in procuring the establishment of a Naval School in the City of Annapolis.

ANNAPOLIS CORPORATION PROCEEDINGS
Tuesday, 10 January 1826

UNITED · STATES · NAVAL · ACADEMY

ANNAPOLIS · · MD

Chronicle

1845

The *Annapolis Corporation Proceedings* records that it is "Ordered that Taney Murray, John Johnson, and Edward G. Tilton, Esq. be requested to proceed to the City of Washington and enquire into the contemplated removal of the Naval School at Philadelphia and if removed to urge in behalf of the Citizens of Annapolis, this as a proper and suitable place for the establishment."

1851

Battery is constructed upon the walls of old Fort Severn at a cost of $6,433.33. To be used for "great gun exercises."

1853

Gas and steam is introduced for heating.

1854

12 July: the Japanese Bell is presented by the Regent of the Lew-Chew Islands to Commodore Matthew C. Perry. Given to the Academy by his widow in 1858.

1855

Second hospital is built at a cost of $13,000.

1860

June: the Herndon Monument is erected by a subscription of officers of the Navy; it is dedicated to the memory of Commander William L. Herndon who lost his life 12 September 1857 while commanding the mail steamship *Central America* in a gallant attempt to save the lives of his passengers.

1861

Academy moves to Newport, Rhode Island, for the duration of the Civil War. Academy grounds transformed into an Army hospital.

1864

From *the Annapolis Corporation Proceedings*: "Ordered that the Mayor, on behalf of the Corporate Authorities, be requested to address a letter to the Hon. Secretary of the Navy urging the re-establishment of the Naval Academy in this City."

1865

11 December: *the Annapolis Corporation Proceedings* records that it is "ordered that the Mayor appoint a committee of seven citizens who shall be requested to take such measures as may be required to secure to this City the continuance of the Naval Academy. . . ."

1867

Water is introduced into the Academy on the completion of the Annapolis Waterworks. Each house in the yard and all the public buildings have hydrants.

1868

24 May: the first service is held in the new [Victorian] chapel.

1869

Summer: New Quarters completed. "There are hot, cold and vapor baths in the Academy for the use of midshipmen, each one of whom is required to take a bath at least once a week. Regular bathing hours are assigned to each gun's crew, which is marched to the bath-house under the orders of its Captain. Each midshipman takes the room assigned to him and is allowed to remain sufficiently long to complete his bath; when the gun captain gives the word 'dress,' as soon as all have complied with that order, the crew is marched out and dismissed. An attendant, for a small consideration from each midshipman, furnishes towels, soap, etc. and keeps the house in order."

There are about 13,000 volumes in the Library, as well as "the best professional and other periodicals published in this country and Great Britain."

1870

Title of "Midshipman" changed to "Cadet-Midshipman" and, for two-year students, to "Cadet Engineer."

1876
Only two of the original buildings of the Army post remain, the Superintendent's Quarters and Fort Severn.

1877
Annex built onto Government House. A further extension constructed in 1887.

1879
Varsity football introduced.

1882
Title changed from "Cadet-Midshipman" and "Cadet Engineer" to "Naval Cadet" for all students.

1892
Varsity track and field teams organized.

1898
Prisoners of the Spanish-American War, including Admiral Cervera, occupy the Old Quarters on Stribling Row in July and August.

1899
Clock tower in New Quarters is condemned and taken down, the bell is erected on the lawn in front of the Dining Hall.

1901
Foundation of Bancroft Hall is laid.

1902
Term "Naval Cadet" is abolished; title "Midshipman" is reinstated permanently.

1905
The remains of John Paul Jones arrive and are placed, with appropriate pomp and ceremony, in a temporary vault.

1906
A picture postcard of Fort Severn carries the message: "Got Mama's letter today. Will answer soon. This is now equipped for our gymnasium but the contracts are out for a new gym."

President Theodore Roosevelt presides over transfer of John Paul Jones's body to Bancroft Hall.

1907
Varsity basketball is introduced.

1909
26 May: demolition of Fort Severn begins.

June Week: the bronze doors of the new chapel are dedicated.

3 July: plans to expand the Naval Academy Hospital are announced.

1910
11 April: Halley's comet is sighted from the deck of the *Santee.*

Old Dennis, who has worked as a maintenance man at the Academy since its founding in 1845, retires.

1912
June Week: Superintendent Captain John H. Gibbons gives the first garden party for the graduating class.

New graduates are commissioned as ensigns for the first time.

30 September: the *Reina Mercedes,* a trophy of the Spanish-American War, arrives at the Academy for a long tour of duty as a station ship.

1913
William Oliver Stevens reports in *The Annapolis Almanack* that on 28 January John Paul Jones is "buried again. Proves that you can't keep a good man down, but six funerals for one corpse is tomb much. Usual number of Paul-bearers."

1914
18 April: the concrete and iron bridge spanning College Creek, built at a cost of $40,000, is "thrown open to the public."

Our Navy and Naval Academy

George Forbes was raised in Annapolis, attended St. John's College (also a military school at that time), and was admitted to the bar in 1894. Today Mr. Forbes is best remembered for The Forbes Collection (housed at the Maryland Hall of Records), a potpourri of photographs, drawings, and articles which illustrated his lectures on historical subjects. The remarks below were delivered before the Sons of the Revolution in the State of New York on 19 April 1916 at Delmonico.

An association of over a quarter century with "Our Navy and Naval Academy" is the justification I offer for selecting it as a lecture subject. True that that association has been altogether social and unofficial, yet I cannot but feel that, with reference to the Academy at least, as the average tour of duty of officers of the Navy attached to the institution is but two years, that I may, with modesty, claim a sufficient acquaintance to speak upon it.

So early as 1802, the Army of the United States was fortunate in having a Military Academy established at West Point on the Hudson, but it was not until 1845 that a naval school was founded. Prior to that time the education of the officers of the Navy had been left primarily to such opportunities as were afforded aboard ship or at scattered points about the country, and it soon became manifest that the chaplains of the men-of-war, who were the instructors, were not competent to teach navigation, ordnance and gunnery, and other naval subjects. Numerous efforts were made by enterprising midshipmen to get the Government to establish a naval school, but without success, until the administration of President Polk, and it was then due primarily to George Bancroft, his Secretary of the Navy, that a Naval School was founded.

When first established, it was known as the United States Naval School. It so continued for five years, when there was a complete reorganization, and it became known as the United States Naval Academy. It has always been located at Annapolis, Maryland, with the exception of the Civil War period, when it was thought expedient to temporarily remove it to Newport, Rhode Island; it was returned to Annapolis in 1865, and with the millions of dollars spent there in recent years, Annapolis may now be safely regarded as its permanent home.

As New York takes a particular pride in its military school on the Hudson, so we Marylanders are proud of the Naval School on the Severn.

The Naval Academy, while under the Navy Department, is under the immediate supervision of its Bureau of Navigation. It is governed by an Academic Staff, consisting of a superintendent, never below the grade of commander, and oftentimes a rear-admiral. He has an assistant, in charge of buildings and grounds, and a naval aide, who is also secretary to the Academic Board. There is also a civilian secretary. An officer known as the Commandant of Midshipmen is head of the Department of Discipline. There are nine other departments, each with a naval officer or civilian professor at its head.

The departments are Seamanship, Ordnance and Gunnery, Navigation, Marine Engineering and Naval Construction, Mathematics and Mechanics, Electrical Engineering and Physics, English, Modern Languages, Naval Hygiene and Physiology.

Officers, professors and civilian instructors, doctors, medical officers and paymasters now number nearly two hundred, but many of these are not members of the academic staff.

Under separate commands, though affiliated with the Academy, are the Naval Hospital and the U.S. Marine Barracks School of Application, both located on the Government Farm near the Academy.

The Naval School started with but two or three dozen boys, and has known nearly a thousand. It began this academic year (1914–1915) with 934. It rarely ends, however, with the number with which it begins, many having been unable to withstand the ordeal of examinations, and as the catalogue considerably puts it, "[they] have been restored to their friends."

The students, after having been called naval cadets, cadets and cadet-midshipmen, are now officially styled "midshipmen," and the words "cadet" or "Naval cadet" are improper, except with reference to the officers of the brigade.

The Acts of Congress dealing with the number of midshipmen and methods of appointment are lengthy, readily available, and need not be here repeated, other than to say that under a recent statute the bar to enlisted men has been let down, several are now enrolled and doing well. It may be well to remark, however, that

Naval cadets in front of the New Quarters [c. 1893]

The class of 1888

candidates must be between the ages of sixteen and twenty; not less than five feet, two inches tall; not less than 111 pounds in weight; and must be unmarried. They sign for an eight years' service and now graduate after four years as ensigns. The pay to each midshipman is $600 a year and if they are good, are allowed $1.00 a month for candy. When deductions, however, are made for clothing, etc, the balance each midshipman receives at the end of the year needs no safe to house it. Before the candidate takes his examination he is required to deposit $280.64. If admitted he is allowed his travelling expenses from his home to the Academy, and if he is not admitted, he gets home the best way he can.

Formerly all examinations for admission were held at Annapolis; now they are held not only at Annapolis, but for greater convenience to candidates, at different points throughout the country. Their mental examination is in reading, writing, spelling, punctuation, capitals, grammar, geography, United States history, arithmetic, algebra and geometry.

Some of the physical requirements are, to the lay mind at least, interesting and diverting, for it is provided that "they must not have decided cachexia, diathesis or predisposition, no unnatural curvature of the spine, or other deformity. They must have at least eight opposing molars, two on each side in each jaw, and they must not have disease of the heart or lungs, or decided indications of liability to cardiac or pulmonary affection, nor must they have had epilepsy or other convulsions within five years."

To expect a would-be midshipman, [one of] the nation's future heart crushers, not to have "a decided indication or liability to cardiac affection" seems to me altogether unreasonable and absolutely prohibitive.

"Is this your 'first engagement' here?"

(Fag Ends, 1877]

The Academy's rifle team

3 December 1909

WHAT DIRECTORY REVEALS

"There are 779 Midshipmen, the Smith family contributing eleven of that bunch; the Joneses were sadly outclassed, having only two representatives of that illustrious family. While there are no churches in the list, and only one Parish, the moral welfare of Midshipmen may be looked after by one Bishop, three Abbotts and one Elder.

"The royalty is represented by four Kings, with only a single Power among them. The 'Queens' can't be counted, as they're only here on hop nights. One Page, two But'ers and one Cook can care for the needs of these sovereigns. (Also, the 'Courts' are in the centre of each wing.) The trades have something to say in the list. Look, there are two Millers, with one Mill, one Baker, one Chandler, one Mason and three Taylors.

"Outdoor life being considered, we have one Hunt and one Chase, the game being a Badger, a Byrd, a Fox, a Wolf, and even a Hogg. One can find innumerable places to look for game: a Hill, a Dale, a Field, a Lott, a Marsh, a Lake and four Moores. A rainbow of colors is presented with seven Browns, three Grays, one Green, one Rose, one White, and one Lavender on the list. (Nothing 'yellow' in the whole brigade.)

"There is one Bieg and one Small, and the latter has a chance for there is a Crow. There is one Long and any number 'short.' In spite of morning inspections, there is one all-day Sleeper and even he got 'papped' for turning in Early. There is one Shine and one Blackwell in the Academy. The blackening is in the corridor boys' boxes. The Midshipmen are able to contribute only two brands of Whitings.

"Although the steam is not turned on until the second Tuesday of Thanksgiving week, we have only one Frost and one Snow. Then we have but one Day and one Knight; also one (not Three) Weeks. We have one Good and a lot better; two Wrights and no wrongs. The 'bread-line' at sick bay every day would hardly lead one to believe that there is but a single Pain in the brigade.

P. S.—There is only one Barr. P. P. S.—There are four Halls but only one 'Rusty Peter.' "

Plebes howitzer drill [c. 1868]

Howitzer formation [c. 1869]

[Fag Ends, 1877]

Artillery drill, Maryland Avenue [1894]

Artillery drill with Nordenfelt revolving quick-firing guns; Fort Severn (background), then the gymnasium, under renovation [before 1893]

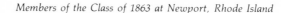
Members of the Class of 1863 at Newport, Rhode Island

During the Civil War the Naval Academy was exiled to Newport, Rhode Island. Officers and upper classmen were quartered in the Atlantic House, *right,* a grandly classical summer hotel. Plebes and youngsters were less fortunate: their homes for the duration were the dark and dreary *Constitution* and the *Santee.* All books, models, and equipment, such as the celestial circle for observing the stars, *left,* that could be transported went with the midshipmen. After the war, there was a campaign among the citizens of Newport to retain the Academy in their city.

At Newport

The Atlantic House, leased by the Naval Academy during its residence at Newport, Rhode Island [1861–1865]

20   *Annapolis during the Civil War, at the time of an expected raid [c. 1864–1865]*

The Academy grounds transformed into an Army hospital [1861–1865]

Hospital tents, Stribling Row to rear [1861–1865]

22   *Surgeon's quarters, commandant's house*

[Following pages] Members of the class of 1870 pose in front of Stribling Row

On 27 April 1861 the Naval Academy was ordered removed from Annapolis, as a part of the Union's effort to ensure Maryland's neutrality. In *The Ancient City*, Elihu Riley records that "by May 13 the Government had a track laid from the Naval Academy, via College Avenue, to the Annapolis and Elk Ridge Depot, and munitions of war were landed at the Naval Academy. . . ." Later the Medical Department of the Army transformed the grounds of the Academy into a general hospital. Fear of a raid by Confederate General Jubal Early motivated the construction of a barricade on Maryland Avenue, *left*, but a steady flow of wounded soldiers was the only evidence of the war that came to Annapolis.

Barricade at the Maryland Avenue gate [1864]

Army hospital officers in front of headquarters [1861–1865]

26

Fountain in front of Blake Row; the second chapel, built in 1868, in background [1872]

Admiral Porter's beautification program [c. 1868]

Devastation of the Academy grounds while they were occupied by the Army during the Civil War inspired Superintendent David Dixon Porter to order a complete renovation. In 1869 an official report boasted that "since the return of the Academy to this place, much has been done in the way of ornamenting and improving that portion of the grounds lying inside the walls; fountains have been erected, roads and paths tastefully laid out, low places filled in, trees, shrubs and flowers planted. The ground in the rear of the Midshipmen's quarters, which was found a barren waste, has been reclaimed, and made one of the ornamental parts of the yard."

Landscaping behind Stribling Row [c. 1870]

Stribling Row consisted of nine buildings constructed in the early 1850s along the edge of the Severn River. After 1869, when the New Quarters replaced it as the primary dormitory for the midshipmen, Stribling Row was known as the Old Quarters.

Steamship engineering building [1870–1871]

Stribling Row [c. 1890]

Buchanan Row

Superintendent's office and library [1873]

Superintendent's residence and official carriage

29

The New Quarters [1893]

NEW MIDSHIPMEN'S QUARTERS.

There is in process of completion a new building designed to accommodate two hundred midshipmen. It is a four story structure with basement, and attic, and is composed of a center building fifty-seven-feet six-inches square, and two wings each one hundred and seventeen-feet nine-inches long, by forty-five-feet three-inches deep; the whole is surmounted by a dome and clock-tower, the latter supplied with a clock having four dials, to be illuminated at night. The base of the dome is surmounted by a promenade gallery, from which a most magnificent view is to be had of the surrounding country and of Chesapeake Bay.

In the basement, under the East wing, there is a kitchen fifty-eight-feet long, by forty-two wide, with large store-room, servants hall &c, attached: under the main building, a pantry; boiler room (for supplying steam with which the building is to be heated,) a coal cellar and a bath room; under the West wing are bath rooms A corridor of twelve-feet in width runs the entire length of the main building and wings while a sixteen-feet hall runs through the main building at right angles to the corridor; there are stairways at the extremities of each wing, and in the main building, these continue to the highest story.

On the first floor, in the west wing there is a mess-hall one-hundred and two-feet long; and occupying the entire depth of the wing, with a store room attached; in the main building, there are four rooms, each eighteen by twenty-one feet, one of which is to be a pantry, one, an office, for the Commandant of midshipmen one, an office for the officer-in-charge, and the fourth, a reception room for visitors. In the west wing there are seven recitation rooms, each twenty-eight by fourteen-feet; and eight water closets. There is the same arrangement of hall, corridors and stairways on this floor as in the basement.

On the second floor the west wing is divided off into twelve domitories; one servants room, and one baggage room, each fourteen by fourteen-feet; the main building into four recitation rooms twenty-one by eighteen-feet each; and the east wing into fifteen domitories of the same dimensions as those in the west wing. The corridors on this and the upper floors run the entire length of the building, the halls and stairways are the same as for the first floor. The wings of the upper stories are the same as the second; the main building in each is divided into five rooms, to be used as recitation rooms &c.

There are entrances in front, rear, and at each end of the building, each covered by a portico. There is a graceful iron veranda extending across the entire front of the building.

A Description and History of the U.S. Naval Academy from Origin to the Present Time [1869]

The New Quarters, so called until the day it was demolished [c. 1893]

With the construction of the New Quarters, photographers had for the first time a vantage point from which to record the ever-changing face of the Naval Academy. The view west, *right*, pictures the armory and natatorium, as well as the doomed settlement of Lockwoodville on Wagner Street, soon to be annexed from Annapolis. On the *following pages*, the view to the east reveals, *from left to right*, the physics and steamship engineering buildings, the gas house, Porter's ornamental gardens, Stribling Row, the lyceum, and the observatory.

View from the New Quarters to Cemetery Point [1882–1886]

[Following pages] View from the New Quarters [1870]

Academics at the Academy included from the beginning much more than book learning. In addition to mathematics, science, history, ethics, English, and modern languages, the midshipmen's curriculum included naval and infantry tactics, navigation, seamanship, gunnery, mechanics, blacksmithing, and woodworking. Courses apparently came and went depending on prevailing sentiments at the Navy Department.

Taking observations with the sextant [1893]

Surveying party [1893]

Experiments in wireless telegraphy, with Professor Nathaniel M. Terry [c. 1910]

[Following pages] Mechanical drawing [1893]

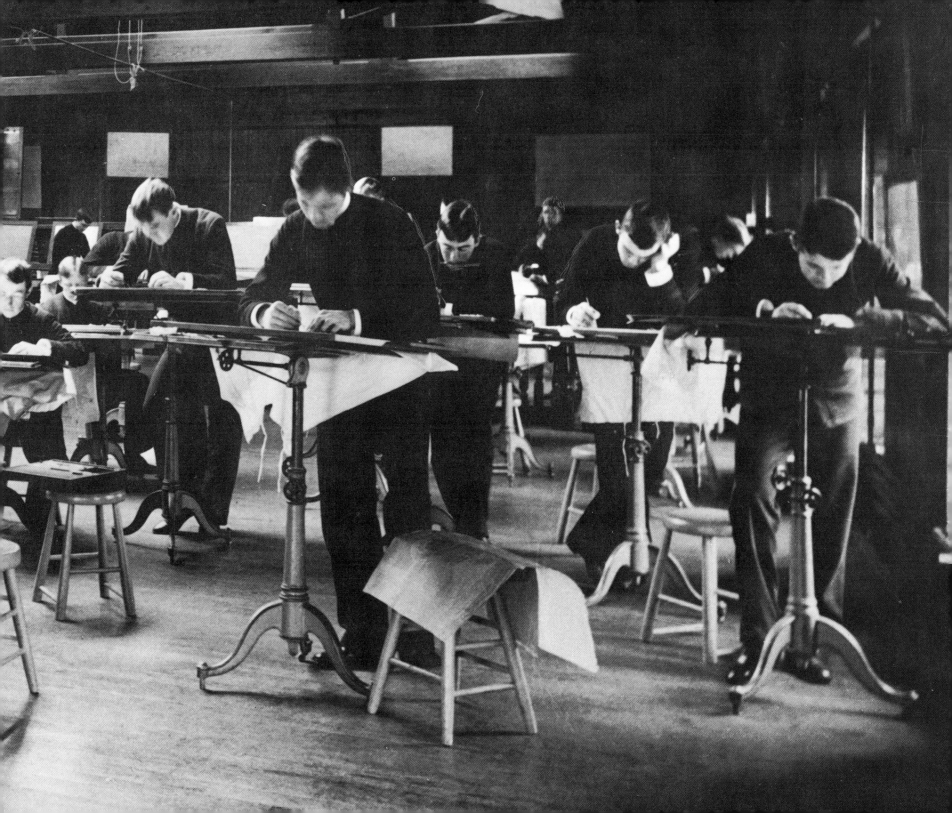

In the armory, Dahlgren Hall

The chemistry laboratory with Professor Paul J.Dashiell

Woodworking shop

Steam engineering [1893]

Testing a torpedo-boat steam engine

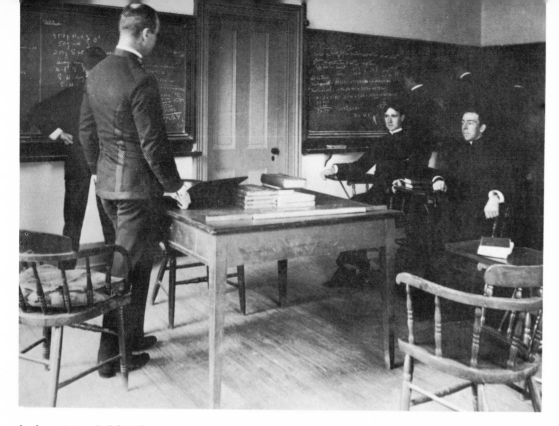

In the recitation hall [1893]

Sneaking a look at the instructor's grade book [1895]

MATH
....AND....
SKINNY

Presented by

The Graduating Class

OF NINETEEN HUNDRED AND NINE

Ceremony June 1 in The Armory—A Revival of Old Custom

The ceremony of "Math and Skinny" by the first class of midshipmen will take place in the Armory at the Naval Academy at 8:30 o'clock Tuesday evening, June 1.

In token of the end of their academic course, it has been customary in the past for the graduating classes of the Naval Academy to present the Burial of Math and Skinny. After a lapse of several years, the custom has been revived by the Class of 1909. This year, however, the subject is not the burial, but the trial and execution of Math and Skinny.

Math is the demon personifying Mathematics, and Skinny that personifying Physics, Chemistry and Electricity.

27 May 1909

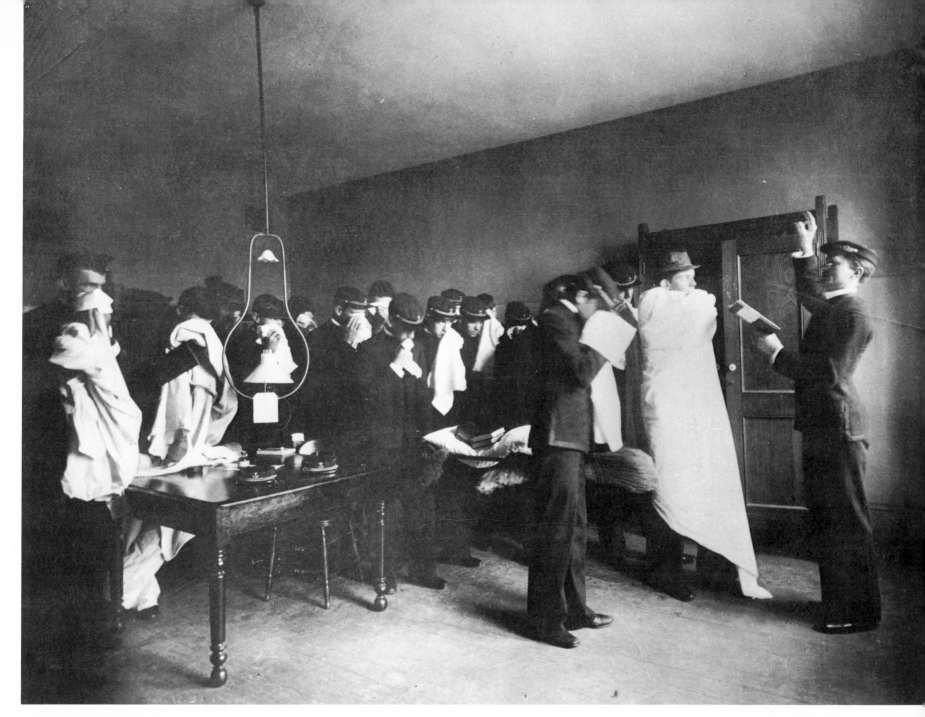

The burial of Math and Skinny

THEY MUSTN'T WHISTLE !

Middies Denied Candy Canteen Also Denied Privilege To Pucker.

"No more whistling in Bancroft Hall," is the latest edict that has gone forth at the Naval Academy. The one-time whistling middies are now silent and there is no more puckering of lips, and merry tunes they were wont to whistle die on the whistler before the puckering can be accomplished.

Bancroft Hall is as silent as the tomb, even as is the last resting place of John Paul Jones who, the middy wag of a few years ago said "lies pickled up in alcohol on a perpetual jag," under the stairway of the home of embryonic admirals.

For midshipman not to whistle is a hardship, but the brigade must grin and bear it.

The candy canteen went last summer while the cruise to "furrin" waters was being made, and no more sweets are allowed sweet middies, and no more soda water and ice cream.

The deprivations to the brigade come not singly, but in whole battalions. Still the midshipmen continue to live.

Recreation hour [c. 1893]

KILLED HIS DEAR UNCLE

Announcement was made at the office of Superintendent Bowyer, of the Naval Academy, this morning that Midshipman Richard Gans Stern, of Philadelphia, had been dismissed from the service. The specifications against Stern are falsehood and obtaining leave by false pretenses, but back of all this is a story that is probably without a match in the annals of the Academy.

Since early in August, young Stern, through the assistance of a young lady between whom and himself there appears to be a mutual admiration society of such strength that departmental rules and other similar small matters were set aside as nothing. The young lady was spending August beside the sea waters at Atlantic City, and Midshipman Stern's desire to join her there was so much her own feeling in the matter that she agreed to aid him in obtaining leave.

A telegram was therefore sent to the young man at the Academy announcing the serious illness of a favorite uncle, whose death bed was likely to be a veritable bed of thorns if he should pass to the great beyond without seeing his middy nephew. The message was signed "Mother" and armed with it the young man easily obtained the leave of absence to hurry to his uncle's bedside.

A week went by and then came another message, this time to the authorities here, announcing the death of the poor uncle, and asking an extension of Stern's leave. This also was granted. When the extension had expired, still another announcement came. This time it was the midshipman himself who was ill. Appendicitis was the trouble and an operation and long rest ; .t off the return to the Academy until September 28.

Upon Stern's return to the Academy it developed that he had an enemy at Atlantic City, who lost no time in squealing on him. As a result he has been dismissed from the service.

Forbidden pleasures [c. 1888–1895]

Mother Goose for Naval Cadets

Sing a song of poker, a pocket full of chips,
Four and twenty middies back from summer trips;
When the pot was opened, the boys began to play;
Wasn't that a pretty game to while the time away;

The boys were round the table counting out their money,
The plebe was in the corner trying to be funny;
One more was in the corridor to fire a warning shout—
Along came an officer and found the whole thing out.

Lucky Bag, 1896

43

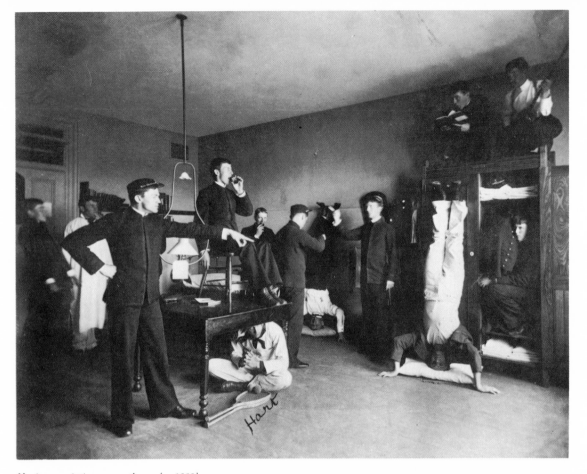

Hazing: variations on a theme [c. 1893]

[Fag Ends, 1877]

ANNAPOLIS 'PLEBE' THRASHES A HAZER

Midshipman Who Finds Upper Classman Maltreating His Roommate Administers Punishment.

[SPECIAL DESPATCH TO THE HERALD.]

ANNAPOLIS, Md., Tuesday.—Persistent rumors of hazing going on regularly at the Naval Academy continue to make themselves heard, and a recent case in which an upper class man fared badly is reported on excellent uthority.

It is understood that one of the largest and most athletic members of the new fourth class administered a severe thrashing to an upper class man who was found in the former's room severely hazing his roommate, a much smaller midshipman. The report has it that the smaller youth was being compelled to do "No. 16" and other exhausting physical exercises known to the traditional hazing code.

According to the story, the larger fourth class man entered his room in Bancroft Hall last night, and found his roommate at the point of exhaustion from the hazing which was being administered to him. He was ordered to perform a similar stunt himself, but his wrath broke through the restraints imposed by the unwritten law of the academy and pitched into the upper classman on the spot.

The upper classman was badly worsted, and is going around with the marks of the combat plainly upon him. It is understood that both the upper classman and the smaller "plebe" were required to seek the dispensary for attention, the latter on account of physical exhaustion due to the hazing.

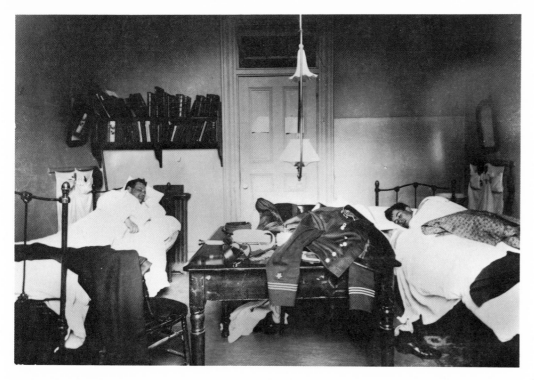

Just before reveille . . .

. . . and just after

"I wish that I knew" groans Plebe,
"What do you want me to do!"

[Fag Ends, 1877]

45

Class of '75.
United States Naval Academy

MINSTREL ENTERTAINMENT.
At the Gymnasium

Saturday Evening, January Tenth,

1874, at Eight o'clock.

COMMITTEE:

C. H. Amsden.   A. C. Hodgson.   C. A. Corbin.
J. S. Manly.   A. Sharp.   W. G. Cutler.

Serious and regulated as were their lives, the naval cadets did find time for, and even ritualized, many playful pranks. Celebration of Christmas Day began with everyone wearing grotesque costumes. Santa Claus, who was the president of the first class, led the procession around the yard, greeting the superintendent and the commandant as they made their way to the armory for an enormous party. Everyone was granted amnesty, no matter how many demerits he had accumulated. Happiest of all, no doubt, was the smallest plebe who, for one day, was the five-striper of the regiment.

Minstrel show [1868]

JOKES OLD AND NEW.

Good Quartette—Ludicrous End Men —But Twenty-Eight Gentlemen in Colonial Costume Compose Chorus—Pleasing Program.

Twenty-eight silk stocking gentlemen, whose calves were more or less shapely and who were dressed in that fetching and graceful colonial costume befitting "Colonial Annapolis," were on view when the curtain at the Naval Academy Auditorium was drawn Saturday evening on "The Masqueraders" in their annual Christmas show.

To be sure it was somewhere near 8.30, and for once the navy did not "mark time," but then everything goes at a "Christmas Show" and beginning late gave the late-comers (and their name was legion) an opportunity to be seated without disturbing the performers, or that part of the audience already seated.

Besides silk stockings, of which there was a knee length display, and costumes of colonial cut in velvet of blue, red, maroon, brown and the like, the chorus also wore white wigs which enhanced its beauty, for this pink-cheeked chorus was handsome to a man. It was also a well-trained chorus and sang melodiously and rhythmically.

After the opening chorus there was an awful shock. Suddenly and without warning the lights went out, and the entire auditorium was in outer (or rather inner) darkness. There was a terrific crash, a tumbling, and the sound of an explosion. It was whispered "the Santee has blown up," or "probably the Hartford."

Someone suggested the financial depression at Bankrupt Hall had caused it to cave in, or John Paul Jones had turned over in his coffin under the stairway for another nap.

None of these horrible occurrences proved to be true, and when the lights were turned on again, they revealed nothing short of a common, every-day occurrence that an aviator had fallen and his aeroplane had been crashed with him (or two of them) beneath. This time it was not Lieutenant Rodgers and Ensign Herbster who had dipped on a slide, downgrade and got their pin feathers wet in the Severn, but it was the so-called Rodgers Bros. (two end men) who had been sailing in the air like other bird men of the navy, and had come to grief, all that was saved of the airship was a jug of bitters, and the first words of the navy aviator as he disentangled himself from the ruins of his airship were: "Wouldn't it be a calamity if all the whiskey were at the bottom of the sea?"

The Christmas carnival [after 1906]

John Paul Jones's casket arriving at Annapolis Roads [23 July 1905]

The corpse [April 1905]

IN PAUL JONES' HONOR

Transfer Of Body To Be Marked With Imposing Ceremony.

THE PROGRAM IS COMPLETE

How President And Other Dignitaries Will Be Received At The Naval Academy On April 24.

[Special Dispatch to the Baltimore Sun.]

Annapolis, Md., April 12. — The authorities of the Naval Academy have completed their part of the ceremonies to be held at the academy on April 24, marking the removal of the body of Admiral John Paul Jones from the temporary tomb in which it was placed on July 24, 1905, to the niche in the memorial room of Bancroft Hall, which has been placed in condition for its reception.

It will remain there until such time as the crypt in the basement of the new chapel is completed, when it will be deposited there with informal ceremony. While the program of events here is complete, Secretary of the Navy Bonaparte is still arranging some of the minor details.

According to the program issued today, President Roosevelt, Secretary of the Navy Bonaparte and a party of diplomats will arrive in Annapolis from Washington shortly after noon on the 24th instant, and they will be officially received in front of the residence of Rear-Admiral James H. Sands, superintendent of the academy, at 12.45 P. M. They will be entertained both before and after the ceremonies.

The President and his party will be met at the railway station by Superintendent Sands and the officers at the head of the departments of instruction at the academy, who will form the escort to the academy grounds. The brigade of midshipmen, the battalion of marines from the barracks and the academy band will take part in the ceremonies. Commandant of Midshipmen Colvocoresses is charged with carrying out the details of the program.

12 April 1906

Reception of the body into the temporary vault [24 July 1905]

TAKEN TO BANCROFT HALL

Impressive Procession Accompanies Body To Resting Place.

The procession to Bancroft Hall started at 4.45 o'clock, upon the completion of the ceremonies in the armory.

Marines from the American fleet, under the direction of a lieutenant, carefully removed the sword and wreaths and raised the coffin from the trusses. They marched with the body behind Chaplain H. H. Clarke down the aisle and out of the northeast door of the big building. Ahead of the Chaplain were three veterans, wearing the regulation blue and carrying wooden canes, whose white locks and bent forms contrasted strikingly with the quick step, straight backs and splendid figures of the sergeant of marines and his eight men who marched close behind them.

Twenty petty officers from the French and American ships followed, merely by way of announcing that the greater men of the two navies were about to approach. Admirals Dewey and Campion walked together, while Admirals Bradford and Davis, the two admirals with the American fleet, completed the quartet.

Aids of the French and American admirals followed, and behind them were the French officers. The academic board was next in line, practically as an escort to the guests of honor.

President Roosevelt and Admiral Sands walked together. Secretary of the Navy Charles J. Bonaparte and Ambassador Jusserand followed, and Governor Warfield and General Porter brought up the rear.

The battalion of midshipmen had preceded the coffin out of the armory and led the way around to the hall, at the entrance to which they were drawn up, the procession passing between their lines. Along the line of march were the cavalry from Fort Meyer, the sailors from battleships and the battalion of marines. Each of these organizations presented arms and stood at "attention" as the body passed by.

As the body bearers reached the main entrance the bugles blew loud and clear, and the spectators stood with hats in hands as the remains of John Paul Jones passed within. Back under the broad marble stairway, in the cleared space provided, the coffin was taken and here placed upon trusses. The President, the French Ambassador, Secretary Bonaparte, Governor Warfield, General Porter, the admirals and others gathered around and listened to the following prayer from Chaplain Clarke:

"Our Heavenly Father, we thank Thee for the memory of the one whom we honor today; for the insight and bravery which he carried to the crowning act of his life— the act that so inspired and strengthened the hearts of the people in their great struggle for nationality. We thank Thee for the sympathy, the material support and the honor bestowed upon him by the great nation beyond the sea.

The remains of John Paul Jones being transferred to Bancroft Hall

ADMIT BEARER AND LADIES.

Ceremonies in Commemoration
of
John Paul Jones,
Armory, Naval Academy,
Annapolis, Md.,
Tuesday, April 24, 1906.
Two o'clock, P. M.

(Right and far right) The president makes his address in Dahlgren Hall

President Theodore Roosevelt arrives

JOHN PAUL JONES ENTOMBED.

A hundred and eleven years after his death, the body of John Paul Jones was yesterday laid in its final resting-place; and in the most appropriate of tombs, beneath the chapel of the Naval Academy.

Annapoils knew John Paul when he was a young skipper. The Academy has been the soul of the navy for which Jones and his compatriots laid the foundation. So long neglected and left to lie in an unmarked grave in Paris, the most famous of our early naval heroes has been thoroughly memoralized since the discovery of his coffin in old St. Louis Cemetery. The body was escorted to America by French and American battleships, received with pomp and ceremony. It is not to our credit that his tomb was not ready and that the coffin lay for years in Bancroft Hall. But that may be forgotten by future generations who will see his bronze statue in Washington, the tablet on the house at Fredericksburg in which he lived, or stand at his long delayed but impressive tomb in the crypt of the Academy chapel. Is it out of place to wish for this god of war entombed in a chapel where officers are dedicated to the country's service in war that he "rest in peace"?--Sunday Sun.

27 January 1913

W is for Wakes; poor John Paul
Every month has a fresh funeraul;
When he's buried at last,
This still may be ast:
Is he the Right corpse after all?

From An Annapolis Alphabet by William Oliver Stevens

Rear Admiral C.R.P. Rodgers's family and members of the faculty [c. 1878]

Officers' baseball team [c. 1895]

Professor William Chauvenet with interferometer [before 1860]

Officers and faculty members attached to the Academy determined most directly the midshipmen's daily experiences, the quality of their education and the degree of discipline to which they would be subjected.

Commander William T. Sampson, superintendent, with family in front of their quarters [1886–1890]

General Sherman and Admiral Porter [1868]

AN INTERESTING QUESTION

Rate of The Class of 1862 Puzzling Officials of Navy Department.

The superintendent of the Naval Academy, officials of the Navy Department and others are interesting themselves over the "rate" of the class of 1862, and its official standing. The members of this class were detached from the Naval Academy in 1861 for special duty at the outbreak of the Civil War, and the Department has been asked whether they are actual official graduates. The matter was referred to Superintendent Sands recently and after investigation it was found that the records contained no information as to their having completed the last term's work and that no certificates as graduates were ever issued to them.

In some quarters, however, it is held that the members of that class are actual graduates, and several of the class are now enrolled upon the books of the Alumni Association of the Naval Academy.

21 May 1907

Commandant Colby M. Chester [1893]

A NAVAL SWIMMING TEST

Assistant Secretary Newberry's alleged suggestion of a swimming test for naval officers, in line with President Roosevelt's order providing for riding tests for army officers, is a topic of general interest in naval circles.

Of course nobody took Mr. Newberry seriously. The suggestion, however, gave food for animated discussion in all the bureaus of the department as to the capacity of naval officers to perform feats in the swimming line or to save their lives if they fell overboard during a storm or through any other accident. One wellknown officer said he thought the capacity to swim should not be regarded as a test of efficiency in the navy. It would be about as effective in the navy, he said, as teaching a railway clerk to jump off a train when a collision is inevitable, so far as the actual benefits that might result.

Officers as well as enlisted men of the navy are taught to swim—the former as part of their course of training at the Naval Academy, and the latter as a result of formal instructions given on the subject by the naval regulations. At the Naval Academy the men are taught both to swim and to dance, thus qualifying them for the water and for the social end of their work. Most of the officers, it is safe to say, can swim, though a number of the older ones would find it pretty hard work to make any sustained effort in that direction.

They have not, however, forgotten their early training in that direction, and are proud of what they have done in that line in their earlier days. The following order, issued March 1, 1900, by Secretary John D. Long, gives the requirements for teaching the enlisted man to swim: "Commanding officers are directed that where the weather, climate and other circumstances will permit, a regular period be established in the routine of exercises and drills for teaching the men and apprentices swimming such exercise to include every enlisted person on board ship, unless excused by the surgeon.

"Commanders-in-chief are enjoined to require compliance with this order to the end that all persons in the service may be expert swimmers, and they will, on their inspections, investigate and report what per cent of the crew can swim."

The officer-in-charge [1893]

Many distinguished military figures have served at the Naval Academy, and their presence has in turn attracted other famous visitors. Rear Admiral David Dixon Porter, first superintendent after the Civil War, greeted many legendary figures during his tenure, among them General William Tecumseh Sherman, with whom he had served at Vicksburg.

5 October 1907

Physical examination [c. 1893]

Old Dennis and friend

The Naval Academy has always been, to a great extent, a self-contained world, having its own heating, lighting, maintenance, medical, and laundry facilities. Among those who kept the systems working was Dennis, *left,* who began his employment in 1845 when the Academy itself began. Classes and buildings and wars came and went, but Dennis remained, for sixty-five years, raking leaves.

A very pressing situation [c. 189

Laundry facilities [c. 1893]

The paymaster's office

The younger generation on Lovers' Lane [before 1900]

School for officers' children

Old Governor Street [c. 1870]

Skaters, behind Steam Engineering building [c. 1868]

Various uniforms, naval and athletic, worn by the cadets [c. 1893]

[c. 1887]

STILL WITHOUT OVERCOATS

A number of inquiries are being made about the midshipmen not wearing overcoats so late in the season. Although there have been some pretty cold days, mercury down to 33 degrees and even one day last week to 29 (three degrees below freezing) the midshipmen have not yet donned their overcoats.

Saturday night the air was cool and keen, and after dancing at the hop in the armory, the midshipmen came out in the cold night air without an extra coat. There are many suffering from colds, some in the hospital, and only a few weeks ago one of the midshipmen died of pneumonia.

It is said the reason for not wearing overcoats so late in the season is the stripes designating the classes to which members of the brigade belong have not been put on the overcoat sleeves, although the tailor shops at the Naval Academy have had the overcoats all summer. That there isn't more illness among the midshipmen is a marvel, as at this season every sane man in the country, be he citizen or military man, is wearing an overcoat and he doesn't have to turn out in the frosty morning air at 6.25 o'clock (as the midshipmen do) either.

19 November 1907

Pleased With the New Order

Everybody who met the midshipmen on the streets in town Saturday noticed that the sailors wore the fatigue uniform. Of course the question naturally arose as to why this dress in town, when one is accustomed to seeing the midshipmen in town in the full dress, tight-fitting jackets, that look so uncomfortable and straight-laced. It finally became whispered around that a new order has been issued at the Naval Academy by Superintendent Badger permitting all the midshipmen to appear in town in fatigue, or "undress" uniform, but they are to wear their full dress when they appear at officer's quarters. The midshipmen are congratulating themselves on the new order, which is one of the most sensible ever issued at the Naval Academy, and they will ever call Captain Badger's name blessed.

7 October 1907

Thanksgiving festival [1867]

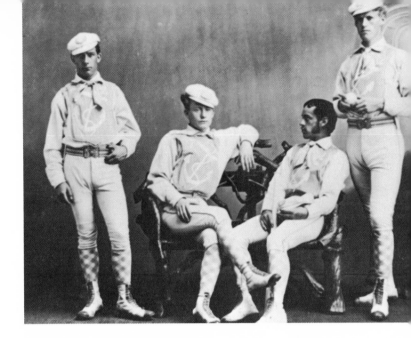

Members of the Essex baseball team [1871]

64

Women's fencing class [1898]

Development of an athletic program was very gradual. It was not until 1865 that a gymnasium was installed in a converted Fort Severn. The same year Swordmaster Antoine J. Corbesier joined the faculty, where he remained until well into the twentieth century. The Thanksgiving Festival was one of the first annual sporting affairs, an occasion recalled by Professor William Oliver Stevens as being "when the cadets chased a greased pig around the field and tried to climb a greased pole as the star events of the day."

Putting the shot, field day

Varsity baseball team [1895]

Lacrosse team [1908]

Varsity crew [1912]

Champion boat club (USS Essex) [1868]

NO TRAINING TABLE?

Uncle Sam Economizing—Middies in a Quandary.

Once in a while the votaries of Uncle Sam are afflicted with an ingrowing case of economy, which is as prevalent as chickenpox or mumps, and as contagious, but not nearly so "dangerous."

It is pretty generally known by the laity that the middies out of their large (?) salaries allowed by the government, pay $20 per month board, which does not seem a great deal, but when taken into consideration that there are approximately 780 midshipmen, is no sum to be sneezed at. At any rate no other institution of learning, so far as can be ascertained, charges near so much for the board and keep of its student body, and many hand out a better class of living than Uncle Sam gives his proteges, even if U. S. is rich, and has no poor relations.

However, whether it be the cost of high living or the high cost of living, it is a fact that recently the board of the middies has been increased $3 per month per capita, and is now $23 instead of $20. Three dollars is not much but when 780 middies pay $3 it means a good round sum of $2,240, enough to keep a printer's devil in ice cream and caromels for many a day.

To be economical, it is understood (not officially) the middies' training table has been cut out. Now, cut out a middies training table and you might as well cut out his tongue, and they do say the crew, that splendid navy crew, positively refuses to row an oar or move a shell on the Severn unless they get a training table.

But there is no affidavit attached to this and the Rocking Chair Brigade will tell.

1911

The Academy's crew [1893]

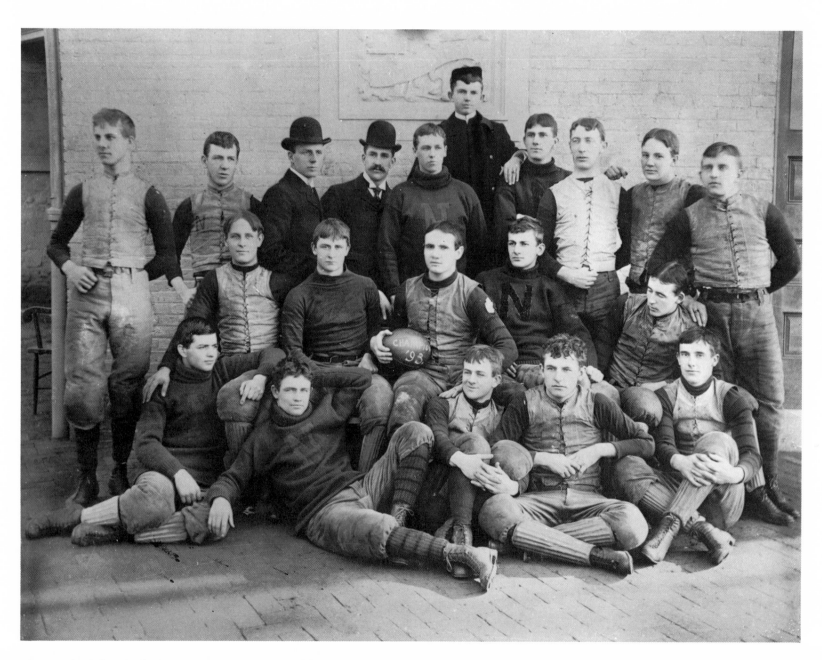

68   *Champion football team of 1893*

Football game at Annapolis [1897]

The grandstand [c. 1894]

A SNAP FOR THE CADETS.

They Have a Picnic With the Team from Johns Hopkins.

[Special to The American.]

ANNAPOLIS, November 2.—A rather one-sided game of foot ball was played here this evening at the Naval Academy between the Cadets and the Johns Hopkins team, resulting in a score of 36 to 0 in favor of the Cadets. In the first inning the Cadets made six touch downs and one goal. The touch downs were secured by C. R. Irvine, R. G. Gartley, R. T. Ritter, Rhum, Latimer, Bailey and Sullivan. The goal was kicked by Williams 26 points.

In the second inning the Cadets made a goal and two touch downs, 10 points. Nydigger and Hicks, of the St. John's team, were umpires. Brown and Whitelock did the best playing for the Hopkins, who only brought the ball once to the Cadets' goal. The Cadets were quite uproarious over their victory.

3 November 1889

Leaving for Philadelphia

THE ARMY INDIGNANT

Superintendent Of West Point Hears Of "Pool" Raised By Cadets

It has been learned in Annapolis that the Superintendent of the West Point Military Academy is highly indignant over the fact that the corps of cadets there raised a pool of something like $3,000, and covered the wager for a like amount made by the Midshipmen at the Naval Academy on the outcome of tomorrow's football battle at Philadelphia

The superintendent did not get wind of the fact until after the money had been placed, and though much against the wish of the authorities, it is understood no action will be taken. For several years the officials at both institutions have sought to prevent betting by the Cadets or Midshipmen, but it has been a custom of years' standing for the rival student bodies to offer a "defi" in support of their team in the great annual game.

Interest in this year's struggle is so keen that the Cadets and Middies waged practically all of the spare cash they had in their jeans.

25 November 1910

ATTACK ARMY WITH SONGS

Middies Preparing To Help Navy In Big Football Game.

The midshipmen of the brigade are now holding regular rehearsals of the songs and yells which they will use in their enthusiasm at the Army-Navy game at Philadelphia on November 30.

Each year the songs, the words of which are to the tune of some popular air, are contributed by different members of the student body and the best ones of the lot are selected for use at the great game. In addition to the brand-new ones, the middies have retained that entitled "Anchor's Aweigh," which made such a hit last season. The words were composed by Midshipman Alfred H. Miles, at large who graduated with the class of 1907, and the words are to the tune of the march dedicated to that class by Prof. C. A. Zimmerman, leader of the Naval Academy Band.

The lines are as follows:
Stand, Navy, down the field,
We'll never change our course,
So, Army, you steer shy;
Roll up the score, Navy,
Anchor's aweigh.
Stand, Navy, down the field,
And sink the Army, sink the Army gray.

22 November 1907

SOCIETY LEADERS VIE WITH NATION'S STARS IN CHEERING

Phalanx of Fair Women Spur on Favorite Warriors

Heroes of the Army and Navy, men of world-wide prominence whose names are enrolled on the historical pages of the Nation; grand dames, equally distinguished as moulders of social history, were to be counted by the score yesterday on Franklin Field.

All affairs of country, State and drawing room were forgotten in the wild enthusiasm of the game. Generals, admirals and statesmen forgot that their silk hats were meant for badges of dignity, and waved them wildly when their favorite side looked good. Stately matrons and graceful debutantes clapped their hands till they ached, and even joined in the cheering.

As a scene, it was a picture-poem of life and color—a huge flower garden, peopled by animated faces, waving golden banners and nodding plumes.

Oliver's Distinguished Party

The fur coat was omnipresent, and the favorite of the hour reaches to the hem of the skirt, with muff and toque to match. Interest, of course, centred around the occupants of the boxes and their guests. Assistant Secretary of War Oliver and his distinguished guests, Mr. and Mrs. Nicholas Longworth and Miss Ethel Roosevelt were the cynosure of all eyes, wrapped from head to toe in luxurious furs.

1 December 1907

NAVY GOAT BESTS BEAR AND MULE

Bewhiskered Pet Looks Wise as Middies Cross Line, While Army's Pair Fail to Prove Mascots

UNDER the gaze of the Nation's fairest women and foremost men, all thrilling with enthusiasm and aglow with color, the Navy yesterday amazed everybody by whipping the Army at football to the tune of 6 to 0.

The odds had been 8 to 5 on the Army, whose splendid showing against Yale and the Indians seemed to augur certain success in the game with the Navy. The Navy has made a poor showing in nearly all its games excepting the one with the State eleven.

Captain Douglas, of the Navy tam, saved the day for the future Admirals. He bucked and bored the line of the opposing team time and time again, and finally, in a spectacular plunge, pushed the pigskin over the goal. The Navy then succeeded in kicking the goal and the deciding score was made.

Across the field the cadets were proudly exhibiting a baby bear, which amused the crowd by standing on its hind legs, and the famous old Army mule that has been in other years part of the Army's traveling show.

If preponderence of mascots meant anything, the game belonged to the cadets.

But the goat only looked wise. As the Navy crossed the goal he winked solemnly. Last night in a stable near the Walton he gravely munched carrots and cabbages, and his gravity was as deep as an owl's.

DEWEY CHEERS WITH MIDDIES

James McCrea, president of the Pennsylvania Railroad, and Charles M. Schwab, one of the steel kings, waved their hats in adjoining boxes. Upon the opposite side of the field Admiral Dewey was giving an exhibition of how to be joyful without becoming excited. He simply sat back, said that he knew it was bound to be, and joined in the deep rumbling siren yell of the middies.

Down upon the field, the middies were wild with joy. One of them danced across the field with the mascot goat. The huge letter "N" formed out of the yellow hats of a number of middies, sitting in such a way as to form the letter upon the background of blue, broke into a sea of waving yellow flags. So wild did the Navy boys become over the touchdown that they threw up the hats, heedless of what became of them.

Before the touchdown, and even afterwards, it was a swift, exciting game. At the outset the Navy smashed and shattered, banged and buffeted the Army line. As Douglas plunged through the line, he left deep, wide gashes in it. Now and then the forward pass was tried by both teams. The Navy seemed to have mastered it better than the Army.

First Army-Navy game [1890]

1915 Army-Navy game

1 December 1907

The Essex, Constellation, *and* Santee *[c. 1893]*

Great-gun exercise—USS Santee *[1870]*

SAW HALLEY'S COMET

**Visible At 3:10 This Morning—Was Seen
By Men On Santee—Entered In Ship's
Log.**

At 3:10 a. m. today, Thursday,
May 5, Halley's Comet was observed
by the crew on the U. S. S. Santee,
at the Naval Academy. When observed the comet was standing East
by South and was at an angle of 45 de-
gres, with the tail up, and eastward of
Venus.

The comet was visible for about an
hour. The fact of its observance exactly as stated above was entered in
the ship's log today on the Santee at
the Naval Academy. The sight was
witnessed by a number of seamen attached to duty on the Santee, and the
Capital is indebted to the ship's crew
for the valued information, which is
official.

It is expected that Halley's comet
will be visible about the same time
here tomorrow morning.

5 May 1910

Quarterdeck of the Santee *[1868]*

ABANDONED BY NAVY

Historic Ship Santee Built Before The Civil War For Which Naval Officers Have Affection.

WILL BE SOLD TO HIGHEST BIDDER

Vessel Recently Sprung Aleak at Naval Academy and Rests on Bottom 12 Feet Below Her Water Line.

The historic old ship Santee, which recently sank at her dock at the Naval Academy, has been abandoned by the naval authorities, and will be sold to the highest bidder with the understanding that he remove her at his own expense.

An inspection of the vessel shows that she is waterlogged and beyond repair for naval purposes. She rests on the muddy bottom of the Severn river with the water about twelve feet above her water line and probably never will float again.

Naval officers have an affection for the old Santee, based on recollections of their student days at the Academy. For many years she was used as a practice ship by the midshipmen, and when no longer able to navigate, was transformed into a prison ship for the embryo admirals who transgressed the rules. In more recent years she was used as a garrison for marines and sailors on this station. A few days ago a large section of her bottom gave way and she sank slowly to the bed of the river.

The Santee is a wooden ship of the square-rigged type. She was built just before the Civil War, but because of a mistake in her design, she never was used or any important service. Tradition has it that the error was pointed out to the designer by his young son soon after the vessel was launched, and that the designer committed suicide by shooting himself on her deck.

The mistake was that the portholes were built directly opposite each other, thus affording an open line of fire to an opposing warship. The Santee was brought to Annapolis in 1865, when the Naval Academy was transferred here from Newport. Soon after that she was dismasted and roofed over. Huge anchors were cast fore and aft to steady her in position and, in fact, for years she practically rested on the soft mud at the Naval Academy dock.

15 April 1912

Interior of the Santee

Santee *[1888–1895]*

Santee Dock

The monitor Passaic [1887–1895]

The yacht America hove down to a monitor

The monitor Passaic on the Severn River. At right, the New Quarters [1887]

A submarine lying off the Academy, with the gas house in the background [c. 1870]

Boat drill under oars [c. 1892]

Sailing drill, steamship Phlox *in background [c. 1892]*

HARPER'S WEEKLY

A JOURNAL OF CIVILIZATION

VOL. XXXVI.—No. 1851.
Copyright, 1892, by HARPER & BROTHERS.
All Rights Reserved.

NEW YORK, SATURDAY, JUNE 11, 1892.

TEN CENTS A COPY.
FOUR DOLLARS A YEAR.

Seamanship drill

Steam launches

Steam launches [1903]

[Following pages] Steam launches transport midshipmen to ships for summer cruises

"Borne away on a three-months lark."

[Fag Ends, 1877]

Saluting the dog

Mr. Midshipman Easy

All aboard

"He could almost throw up his commission."

[Fag Ends, 1877]

Midshipmen Nimitz, Stewart, and Ingersoll swab the deck

Billy goes cruisin'

[Fag Ends, 1877]

Seamanship drill [1896–1897]

The New Naval Academy

Not only on the mighty floating fortresses that from year to year slide down the ways in our ports on the Atlantic and the Pacific, but also on the new Naval Academy at Annapolis, rests Uncle Sam's hope for future mastery of the seas. Just as the greatness of a city is not in its buildings, but in its citizens, so the power of a navy is not alone in its armor-belts and armament, but in the men who command its squadrons and who fire its guns. Twenty-thousand-ton battle-ships will outlive their usefulness in fifteen or twenty years, but the great nautical school on the banks of the Severn river—a vast pile of granite and marble—will house for generations the future captains and admirals of the United States Navy. During the present year all the buildings will be completed, and the scheme quietly outlined by naval experts a decade ago will be realized. At a cost of more than twelve million dollars America will possess a naval academy unmatched by that of any other nation—an imposing architectural monument, and a training school so arranged and equipped as to secure a maximum of convenience and efficiency.

To the visitor who comes into Annapolis Harbor the first view of the buildings is impressive. Rising above a high sea-wall, and running parallel with it, is Bancroft Hall, the midshipmen's quarters; and adjoining this, on the right and left respectively, are the boat-house and the armory—a combination of buildings presenting an unbroken front of twelve hundred and seventy feet, one of the longest in the world. Directly in front is the semi-circular harbor, deep and broad, while on the boat-house side flows the Severn—an arm of the Chesapeake Bay. Behind the armory, and towering over it, is the Chapel, whose dome can be seen far down the Chesapeake. Around the lovely campus in the rear are the superintendent's residence, the Administration Building, Sampson Row—the professors' homes—the new Naval Hospital, the Academic Building, the power-house, and the Marine Engineering and Naval Construction Building.

Between the sea-wall and Bancroft Hall stretches the new parade ground, as level as a floor—made so by filling in with more than two hundred thousand cubic yards of earth. This great rectangular campus is eighteen hundred feet long and six hundred and eighty feet wide—larger by one-third than the old parade ground, and large enough to give ample space for the most elaborate practice and exhibition drills.

Entering the Academy enclosure—a high wall runs around it except on the two water sides—the visitor is impressed anew with the size and scope of the architectural scheme and the regal beauty and newness of the buildings around him. The immense campus, perfectly kept, and shaded by hundreds of fine old trees, sweeps off toward the Severn, whose waters glisten through the branches. Bancroft Hall and its great wings loom up even larger than from the front. The buildings at the back, invisible from the water, would make a commodious academy in themselves.

The new chapel, its yellow dome gleaming above the tree-tops, dominates the whole. The edifice was designed as a memorial to the heroic dead of the United States Navy, and the corner-stone was laid by Admiral Dewey in 1904. In the magnificent mausoleum, scarcely excelled by that of Napoleon at the Invalides, in Paris, will rest the remains of John Paul Jones. While the building is receiving its final touches the body of the first of our naval heroes lies in Bancroft Hall.

No suggestion of doubt seems to have caused the slightest uneasiness in naval circles and the work of completing the sarcophagus goes on. When it is finished there will be a great gathering at Annapolis to fire a salute over the final resting-place of the famous captain of the *Bonhomme Richard.*

The chapel itself has caused no little discussion among architectural critics. The main structure, of blue-gray granite and firebrick, is almost square, measuring one hundred and fifty by one hundred sixty feet. The dome is covered with gold, and all around it stand out in high relief decorations of crossed swords, guns, and other war-like insignia. The effect is certainly novel and bold: "surprising" and even "staggering" are words that have been applied to it by visitors. Some of the irreverent midshipmen call it "Wiegard's Wedding Cake," after a merchant of local fame who owns a sweetmeat shop in the town. It must be admitted that the yellow dome strikingly resembles a big wedding cake with ornamental icing over the top.

The armory was the first of the new buildings for which ground was broken. It is of solid granite, and measures one hundred and ten by four hundred and ten feet. Most of this ample space is occupied by a great drill hall, with galleries, recitation rooms and dressing rooms. In the armory are stored trophies of the triumphs of the Stars and Stripes on sea and land. There are cannon captured

The construction of Bancroft Hall [1901]

View of the armory from the chapel

in the Tripolitan War, and wooden guns taken from the Filipinos. In the gallery are models of present-day projectiles and subtarget guns for practice. The aiming of an empty target rifle registers a hypothetical shot on the wall opposite.

The boat-house, which is of exactly the same size as the armory, contains dozens of big whale-boats in which the midshipmen practice on the Severn every fine afternoon.

Like Bancroft Hall, the new Academic Building is a central hall connecting two wings, measuring in all, three hundred and seventy by four hundred and forty feet. Situated at the far end of the campus, it is surrounded with old cannon, some of which were used in the wars of two and even three centuries ago. The class-rooms are arranged with minute care as to comfort and facilities for accurate and rapid work. In the large library are thousands of volumes pertaining to every phase of maritime activity. The lecture hall—shaped like a section of a globe—seats a thousand people.

Northeast of the Academic Building is the powerhouse, with its machine-room, testing-plant, and battery-rooms, generating three thousand horse-power for heating and lighting all the buildings on the grounds. Nearby is the Marine Engineering and Naval Construction Building, containing pattern-shops, machine-shops, model-rooms, drawing-rooms, laboratories, and nine recitation rooms.

The imposing Naval Hospital, across the way, has just been opened. It is equipped, of course, with the most modern surgical appliances. One department is used exclusively for operating the X-ray machines. The interior of this room is black, with ruby lights—these colors aiding the use of the X-ray. A hydrotherapy room is another feature.

Sampson Row, named in honor of the late Rear-Admiral Sampson, is composed of handsome three-story dwellings, the homes of the professors at the academy. The buildings run down to the water's edge, affording a fine view of the high bluffs far up the Severn.

The entire plan, says *Munsey's,* has been worked out by Uncle Sam without the blaring of trumpets, and most visitors to Maryland's attractive little capital city, which is situated about thirty miles from either Baltimore or Washington, know little of the magnificence of the academy buildings until they pass the guard at one of the enclosure entrances.

Littel McClung
The Evening Capital Historical and Industrial Edition,
May, 1908

Porter Row [c. 1908]

Colonel Robert M. Thompson, Evelyn B. Longman, and Ernest Flagg

U. S. Naval Academy
Annapolis. Md.
Oct. 25 1869.

Order:

Midshipman Thompson (1st class) who plays so abominably on a fish horn, will oblige me by going outside the limits when he wants to practice or he will find himself coming out of the little end of the horn.

David D. Porter
Vice Admiral
& Supt. N. A.

WOMAN GETS THE PRIZE.

Her Design Accepted For The Naval Academy Bronze Doors.

By the unanimous decision of the judges, says the New York Times, in the competition for the bronze entrance doors for the United States Naval Academy, the first prize was awarded to Miss Evelyn B. Longman. The judges were Col. Robert M. Thompson, Daniel C. French, Ernest Flagg, Walter B. Chambers and Charles Grafly. The doors are the gift of Colonel Thompson as a memorial of the class of '68.

There were in all thirty competitors, but Mr. French said that the judges had little difficulty in arriving at a decision and that all agreed, without hesitation, that Miss Longman's work merited the prize. "Miss Longman's achievement in winning this competition," he added, "has been equaled by few, if any, sculptors of her sex in this country. Her success did not surprise those who are familiar with her previous work, for in several instances she has given evidence of great ability. Perhaps the best-known work is the figure 'Victory' in the Festival Hall at the St. Louis Exposition. Miss Longman's design is divided into two main groups, representing "Peace" and "War." In the former, on the left portal, an old man, symbolizing "Science," is in the act of explaining a problem to students in the garb of the Naval Academy. One youth holds in his right hand a model of a man-of-war, while under his left is a draughtsman's triangle.

The doors, with the transom and space above, are to be approximately 21 feet in height and 10 feet wide.

In the group "War," which adorns the right portal, a female figure typifies "Patriotism." A coat of arms shows beneath her draperies. One clenched hand rests upon a cannon; the other points to the distance, where rise the masts of ships, toward which the naval cadets in the background are marching. A young man who is about to take his place at her side represents the response of youth to the call of patriotism.

Dedication of the chapel doors [June Week 1909]

The gentlemen flanking sculptress Evelyn Longman (who was, by the way, 19 years old at the time), *far left,* also were among the celebrities at the Academy on 2 June 1909. Colonel Robert Means Thompson, who distinguished himself by his lack of musical talents while a member of the Class of 1868, was the donor of the new chapel's magnificent bronze doors. Indeed, it was he who encouraged the construction of the new Academy by hiring eminent architect Ernest Flagg (on Ms. Longman's left) to propose a master plan.

Thompson also formed the Naval Academy Auxiliary Athletic Association in 1891, thereby playing an active role in the promotion of sports. Thompson Stadium was named in his honor.

The Passing of Fort Severn

I n the demolition of the old building at the wharf of the Naval Academy will disappear a structure of some historical interest. Old Fort Severn, an Army post from 1808 to 1845, which entered into the military service of many patriots during the war of 1812 and subsequently, will soon pass out of existence. The place was a noted one before going into possession of the national government for military use, the entire water front of the Naval Academy having been fortified during the revolution, and it was here that continental troops were embarked en route between the north and the south, and here was Pulaski's legion formed.

On the point a windmill was built of stone about 1760, and the walls were included in those of the fort. A relic of colonial days nearby, from 1845 to 1883, was the residence of the superintendent, but in the latter year it was condemned as unsafe and demolished. This building was erected by John Duff, an architect, prior to 1750, and was occupied as the residence of the Dulany family of lawyers who were the recognized leaders in the profession down to 1808 when it became the residence of the successive commanders of the fort. It was on the shore west of the fort that the brig *Peggy Stewart* was run ashore and burned in October 1774, for bringing tea into the colonies. Her owner, Andrew Stewart,* applied the torch to appease the indignant citizens.

In 1808 the government erected Fort Severn on the site of the old mill and ten heavy guns were mounted, which, with those of Fort Madison on the north side of the Severn, was the main defense of the water front. Nine or ten acres was the extent of the grounds. Besides the commander's house were officers' quarters and barracks for a small detachment of troops, but during the War of 1812 the numbers varied from a company to several hundred, as the exigencies of the service demanded. It is known that detachments of Maryland and District volunteer and military companies and the Thirty-sixth United States Infantry, Col. Henry Carberry, largely recruited in the District, saw service here.

Included in this regiment were the companies of Capts. Thomas Carberry and Thomas Corcoran, recruited to the Seventh United States Infantry in 1815. Though the guns of the Fort were never fired at an enemy, on more than one occasion they were shotted ready for the approach of the enemy's vessels. For saluting purposes, however, they were often fired, for it was here that Lafayette was honored on his visit in 1824, and diplomats and other dignitaries of foreign nations en route to the capital coming on vessels of war, the interchange of salutes with the fort was not unusual. Until 1845 it was garrisoned, and in August of that year the troops, a single company, marched off with the drum and fife playing "The Girl I Left Behind Me" to a steamer which bore them to another post, many Annapolitans giving them a send-off.

Efforts had been made at times for thirty years or more for the establishment of a naval school or academy in the place of the dozen schools for educating midshipmen in navy yards and on men-of-war. William Jones, of Pennsylvania, Secretary of the Navy, who by virtue of his service in the navy of the revolution, foresaw the expediency of such a school in November 1814, urged it on President Madison. From this time on, efforts were made for congressional action, without success. In 1825 the subject was before Congress, and the following year the Maryland legislature adopted resolutions presenting Annapolis as possessing superior advantages for the site of such a school. The lack of one vote in the Senate killed the project at that time.

In 1845, George Bancroft, Secretary of the Navy under Mr. Polk, took up the subject, found means to establish the school, and enlisted the assistance of the board examining the midshipmen that year. The board reported in favor of Fort Severn, and, Commander Franklin Buchanan having been appointed superintendent, the transfer was made. The school was opened October 10 following, with but three professors. The Academy grounds proper have increased from nine to fifty acres, and the hospital and other grounds outside the walls contain over a hundred acres more. From a few dozen its roster has increased to eight hundred names. Many will revere the spot because of its associations with colonial and local history before its use by the Academy.

The Evening Capital
2 October 1909

Fort Severn before the Civil War, with guns still in place

* Anthony Stewart

THE WART MUST GO

22 May 1909

Fort Severn Gets Reprieve

Orders have been issued at the Navy Department for the demolition of Fort Severn at the Naval Academy. A decision was reached that this should be done shortly after Assistant Secretary of the Navy Winthrop returned from his visit here. The work of destruction will not begin immediately, however. The orders which have been issued direct that before beginning work those in charge at the Naval Academy shall make an estimate of the cost of the work and the time it will take to finish the job.

26 May 1909

PROTESTS CAME TOO LATE

Portions of Old Fort Severn Being Torn Down

From the present outlook it appears that protests from ex-Governor Warfield and other patriotic Marylanders against the demolition of Fort Severn at the Naval Academy have been without vail. Ex-Governor Warfield's letter reached Secretary of the Navy Meyer Saturday morning and was promptly answered.

The former Governor was informed that as there appeared to be no sufficient reason why the old ruins should be allowed to remain as a hindrance to the work at the Academy they had been ordered razed and the work was already under way. The demolition of the building, however, has not been completed so far as the brick work, and the original foundation is standing today. It is not too late to save this and could, at small cost, be covered with a platform, mounted with old guns, and appropriately marked with a tablet to indicate its historic significance.

The people of Maryland do not approve of the decision of the Navy Department, according to Governor Warfield. After inquiring as to the accuracy of the reports that the fort was to be pulled down, Mr. Warfield said: "As a native of Maryland and as an American citizen who wishes to see preserved and marked all historic buildings and places, I wish to enter my earnest protest against such unpatriotic action."

27 May 1909

PLEA FOR FORT SEVERN

Mr. George Forbes Writes To Secretary Of The Navy

Among those who have also written to the Secretary of the Navy protesting against the tearing down of old Fort Severn is Mr. George Forbes, who also wrote to the Navy Department and to Senator Rayner protesting against the destruction of the fort.

Mr. Forbes declares that to remove this old landmark will be nothing short of vandalism. He said that he has lived here twenty-five years, and he regards it as important and desirable that Fort Severn should be preserved intact. The present fort, he said, was built in 1808. Previously the site had been occupied by an old windmill, which was constructed in 1760.

"It is the only remaining building of the post of Fort Severn and the old naval school," writes Mr. Forbes, "affording thereby a delightful contrast to the modern institution."

16 June 1909

CALLS FORT SEVERN A WART

What Capt. Bowyer The New Superintendent Thinks of Historic Fort—Says It Should Have Been Moved Long Ago

Capt. John M. Bowyer, the new superintendent of the Naval Academy, made his first official visit to the Navy Department, Washington, yesterday.

He told Secretary Meyer, Assistant Secretary Winthrop and Rear Admiral Pillsbury that the work of the summer season has been well started. Nearly all the officers newly detailed have reported for duty at the Naval Academy, and the members of the new fourth class are reporting for entrance.

Captain Bowyer was interested in the report of the board of visitors and expressed the hope that the most important recommendations would be adopted. The work of razing Fort Severn had been begun and the superstructure removed. The formal order for the complete demolition of the fort will probably be issued today.

The fort as it stands is "a wart on the face of the Academy grounds," the new superintendent said, and should have been removed years ago.

19 June 1909

OLD FORT SEVERN DOOMED

Assistant Secretary Winthrop Suggests a Tablet For Historic Site

In spite of all protests made by historical associations and private persons against the demolition of old Fort Severn, in the Naval Academy, the Navy Department will not modify its orders for the removal of the ancient relic. Assistant Secretary of the Navy Beekman Winthrop has written a letter to Senator Rayner setting forth very frankly the position of the department.

"I am heartily in accord with any movement to retain structures and institutions of historical interest," he writes. "I do not believe, however, that the present Fort Severn is of such value historically as to justify the department in authorizing the large expenditure of money which would be necessary to restore it to its original condition. It was constructed, I believe, in 1803, but never fired a hostile shot and was never fired at.

"In the process of converting the old fort into a gymnasium in the early days of the Academy, the walls, originally nine to ten feet thick, were blasted out, leaving only a thin outer shell. The upper part of the fort was removed and the steel and wood superstructure erected. This has recently been taken down. All the guns and carriages were removed long ago, and all that remains is a low, circular brick structure, which has but little resemblance to the old fort. I believe that a tablet marking the space formerly occupied by the fort will be much more in keeping and fully as desirable from a historical point of view as to retain the present structure."

Mr. Winthrop has not yet heard from any sources concerning his suggestion for a memorial tablet.

21 June 1909

Last Hope For Saving Old Fort Severn Must Go

LETTERS TO THAT EFFECT

Department of the Navy,
Washington, D. C., June 17, 1909.
My Dear Mr. Carpenter:
In reply to your letter of the 15th instant, enclosing a telegram from Gordon H. Claude, Mayor of Annapolis, I have the honor to inform you that I have taken up the matter of Fort Severn with the President and he agrees with me that, taking into consideraton its present condition and location, it would be inadvisable to restore the fort.

Faithfully yours,
G. L. MEYER,
Secretary of the Navy.

Navy Department,
Washington, D. C., June 17, 1909.
Dear Sir:
In reply to your letter of June 15th, transmitting a copy of the preambles and resolutions adopted by the Mayor, Counselor and Aldermen of the City of Annapolis at a meeting held June 14, I have the honor to inform you that the Department, after a careful consideration of the present condition and location of the fort, has decided not to restore the same.

Very respectfully,
BEEKMAN WINTHROP,
Acting Secretary.

Baltimore, Md., June 18, 1909.
Mr. Philip E. Porter,
City Clerk, Annapolis, Md.
My Dear Sir:
I have your favor of June 15th enclosing copy of resolution adopted by the Mayor and City Council of Annapolis on June 14th, protesting against the removal of old Fort Severn.

I have for a long time been making every effort with the Secretary of the Navy to effect a reconsideration of the expressed policy of the Department to tear down Fort Severn, and I have this day forwarded to him the resolution which you sent to me, asking him to give the same his favorable consideration.

Yours very truly,
JOHN WALTER SMITH.

Tearing Down Old Gym

The work of tearing down the old gymnasium at the Naval Academy has begun. The old gym was built upon the foundation of Old Fort Severn, and it is genreally understood that after the gymnasium proper has been razed the original foundation of the old fort will remain and be mounted with guns. The old Fort Severn is one of the most historic spots in the Naval Academy and attracts many visitors.

26 April 1909

Fort Severn converted into a gymnasium [c. 1895]

Fort Severn from the Severn River [c. 1904]

Interior of the gymnasium [before 1909]

[Preceding pages] Color Girl Parade under the old mulberry tree

Color Girl Parade [before 1903]

Since 1871 one of the highlights of graduation week festivities has been the Color Girl Parade. Over the years the tradition has changed remarkably little: the honored favorite of the color company commander dons a white gown, transfers Old Glory to the deserving color company, and, for her trouble, receives a well-witnessed kiss.

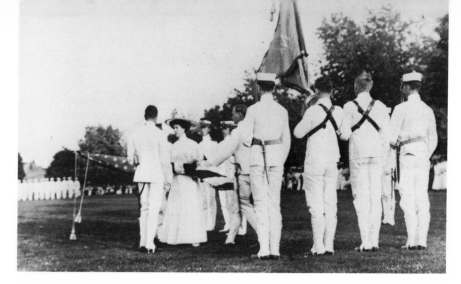

Presentation of colors [1908]

Emily Stewart, the cynosure of the Color Girl Parade in 1892

Sir   Washington City 25th Jan 1846
        Having understood that you were in want of
a Bugler at Annapolis, I have availed myself
of this method of making application for the situation, (provided) we can agree upon the terms, I
have also a Boy who is an excellent Drummer—and
is well used to all kinds of Tunes and calls used
in the U States Service as also, myself on the Bugle.
If you should think proper to notice this com-
munication, you will please state distinctly your
terms—
        I should be very glad if the Boy could
be employed as I am his Father—and shall be
anxious to have him with me; as it is unnecessary
to say more until I hear from you, I therefore
subscribe myself
                        Very Resp.y your Ob.t Serv.t
S. B.   Patrick McGreevy
        hiss Address to my name, Navy
Yard, Washington City, D C

The hospital band during the Civil War

Dress parade, with drum major Old Denver leading the band [c. 1870]

The Naval Academy Band at the bandstand on Chapel Walk [before 1902]

By 1869 the Naval Academy Band was composed of twenty-eight members. It was required to play every morning and evening for one hour and for drills and dress parades. Many of the musicians also played reed and string instruments and formed a fine orchestral band for hops and balls.

Bandmaster for more than 25 years, Charles Zimmerman joined the Academy band as a trumpeter at age 14 [c. 1905]

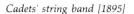
Cadets' string band [1895]

Gathering [1896]

PROMENADE TO MUSIC

Middies Pleased At Evening Band Concert.

Every midshipman who enjoyed the band concert in the Naval Academy grounds Saturday evening and nearly the entire brigade was scattered in groups about the grounds, expressed himself well pleased at the music and the privilege afforded them of promenading the grounds with their friends.

The idea of a promenade concert was conceived by the Naval Academy Young Men's Christian Association, under whose auspices it was given, after the Academy authorities granted permission. The Naval Academy band played at the old band stand in front of the Superintendent's quarters. The program of music arranged by Lieutenant Zimmerman was pleasing and of the lighter music and popular airs, which everybody enjoyed.

Many young lady friends of the Midshipmen enjoyed the promenade concert which lasted from 8 to 9 o'clock, and despite an occasional shower, or passing rain cloud, all were well pleased with the music and the recreation and diversion it afforded.

25 April 1910

Parade in front of the Marine barracks (on the site of Dahlgren Hall) [1893?]

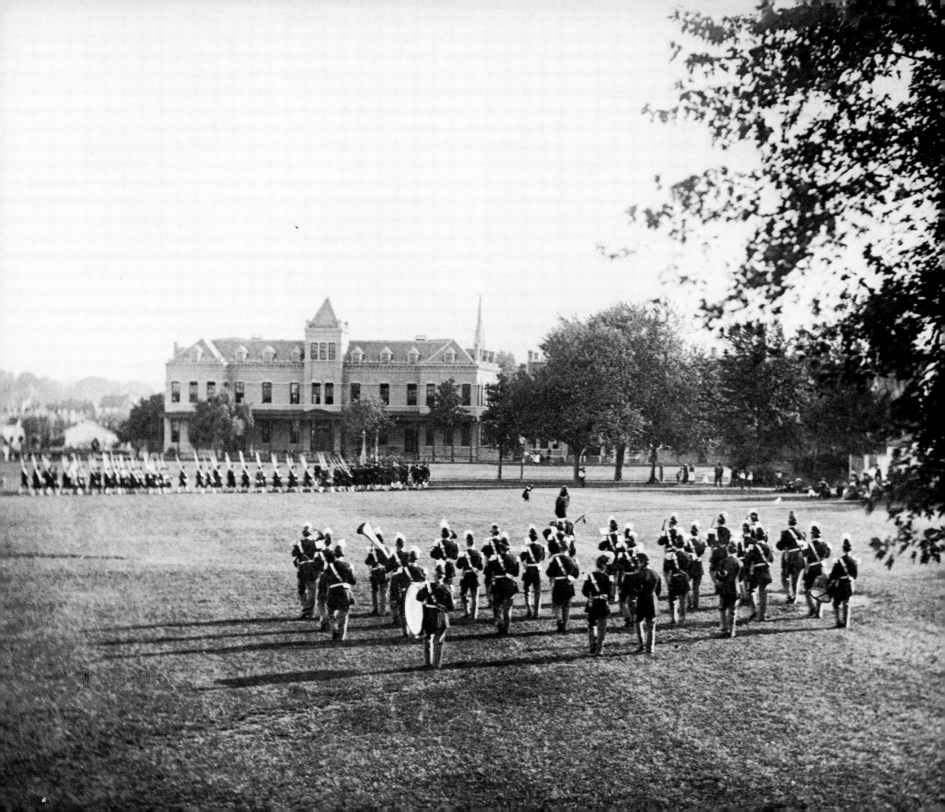

The first ball

"Washington beauties there, by the score,"
Vie with the belles of Baltimore."

[Fag Ends, 1877]

The Naval Academy Ball, 8 January 1869, sketched for Harper's Weekly

From its earliest days, the Academy encouraged the development of the social graces. The first ball *(above left)* was held when the Naval School was but three months old and was "numerously attended by ladies and gentlemen from various parts of the union," according to the report of the midshipman officer the following day. Soon, getting an invitation to a naval ball or to a hop, which was less formal and held more frequently, was considered an honor. Year after year, the daughters of naval officers living in the yard, young women of Annapolis, and not a few debutantes from Baltimore, Washington, and beyond, swirled with their eager escorts around the transformed dance floor of the camouflaged armory or gymnasium.

NAVAL ACADEMY BALL AT ANNAPOLIS.

THIS ball, of which we give an illustration on page 72, was given on the evening of January 8, by the first-class cadets of the Annapolis Naval Academy. The preparations were elegant and elaborate, involving great expense, and the result was a magnificent success. The number of cadets was about ninety; their class is for the most part made up of wealthy young men. The relatives of the boys, and a large number of beautiful girls, honored the occasion with their presence. The interior of an old fort was transformed by these merry-makers into a fairy-like paradise. The roof was lined with blue and studded with silver stars; the sides were ornamented in the best artistic style, cutlasses and muskets being profusely distributed amidst a vast quantity of bunting and evergreens, the whole presenting a very charming *tout ensemble.* Admiral PORTER was present with his son, Captain D. E. PORTER.

Where Every Girl's A Belle

There may be scenery along that two-hour trolley ride as persistently picturesque as the back-drop in a rustic drama, but I didn't see it. Going down to Annapolis in June Week, you instinctively turn your back on car-window views; in fact forget everything in life except the carful of girls.

Girls of every sort they are: blonde girls, brunette girls; tall girls, short girls; thin girls, fat girls; dainty girls in dainty frocks, trig girls in tailored linen suits; girls in hats that come down like a candle-snuffer and girls in hats like wide-thrown haloes.

But all embody the very spirit of youthful energy, and all are so pretty that it is difficult picking the prettiest.

There are, it may incidentally be remarked, many suit-cases and some chaperons in the car; but these constitute, of course, merely the stage properties in the scene.

No need to search your car window to catch the approach of your destination, either, for as the first dim outlines of that quaint, low-lying Mecca are picked out on the horizon by the June sunshine, that carful of girls suddenly takes on a new sparkle.

Cheeks grow a shade pinker, eyes a trifle brighter. Lips are parted, but not in conversational explosives, for the conversations, subdued or animated, that have been in steady progress, end quite suddenly—even the bewitching chatterbox who has been talking and shrieking with pleasure at her own sayings subsides with an excited giggle.

Then an athletic-looking girl—the type who would, you are sure, play the piano with the same enthusiasm and technique with which she would play basket-ball—reaches up and swings her suit-case into the aisle as if it were a bag of fudge, just to give expression to suppressed emotion.

The spell is broken; the car flutters; frocks are smoothed, hats straightened, parasols shaken. Vanity-cases appear and mighty pretty preening absorbs that carful of girls.

"You must tell me what my duties are," I say to Margarita a little nervously.

"The first duty is to forget that you are on duty," my charge chirps saucily, but she goes on, dimpling: "You'll have such a good time yourself that it won't be hard. The Academy really chaperons. Chaperons aren't chaperons here. They're belles too."

A little pink-and-white novice asks:

"Is it like any college commencement?" And a very splendid girl, who carries herself like one who is the only daughter in her father's house, replies:

"About as much as a summer hotel piazza is like the fun of being the girl at an army garrison. No matter how insignificant you are before you come, afterward they make you feel as if the world couldn't stagger along without you. And there are so *many* of them!" she finishes ecstatically.

The naval officer's wife who is bringing this goddessy young woman down as her guest tries to sound reproving as she warns:

"But it's not going to be middies morning, noon and night, this year, Barbara. You *must* discourage a few. It's too hard on me and—the parlor furniture!" she laughs.

Then we are at the first stopping-place within Annapolis limits, and instantly some dozens of middies have boarded the car. They file in with splendid dignity, but a boyish elation shows in their smooth, frank faces.

They are obviously tickled to have arranged their liberty so as to reach the farthest outpost. Soon they are bending above certain seats, and you catch occasional glimpses of those girls' frocks through a barricade of blue uniforms.

At every stopping-place we acquire similar delegations of eager middy hosts, and when at last we reach Carvel Hall—that grim Colonial landmark transformed into a rambling hostelry that is almost always overrun with youths and gaiety—a last batch of waiting uniforms advances rapidly.

And out of the confusion of disembarking and greeting, every lassie emerges with her laddies by her side, or less poetically stated, there appear from two to five middies in the train of each girl in this spectacle of youth and devotion.

The repetition of the maid-and-middy group is seemingly without end, and I realize that other cars and other means have been bringing girls and girls into this sleepy old town—a perfect avalanche of girls has descended; yet the lads outnumber them.

And such lads! Soldier-straight and built like a wedge, from broad shoulder to ankle, yet with the elasticity that bespeaks strength and freedom of youth: clear-eyed boys to be proud of.

Margarita has two claimants: a tall, lean, brown boy, and a square boy with red hair and the friendliest kind of smile. I am introduced to these two, and they do not make me feel that a velvet

107

Members of the class of 1903 and friends on Lovers' Lane

On Porter Row

Watching the games [c. 1892]

gown and soft food will shortly be my portion, as is sometimes subtly conveyed to chaperons.

But my protegee looks a shade disappointed.

"Ben's on the grade," announces the tall boy, and I detect a slight gleam in his serious eyes.

"Then we'll go right up to the grounds," declares Margarita.

"Without lunch?" asks the ruddy-haired middy, pretending to inhale an enticing aroma. He is a cousin.

Margarita, however, is adamant, and in a very few minutes we are on our way toward the Academy grounds.

"On the grade" is explained to me as signifying disciplinary restriction of a middy's activity to the grounds. None but a thinking-machine, it seems, could escape from being "on the grade" sometimes, slight offences accumulating as inevitably as "spots on your blouses," to quote the frank cousin.

Ben's climax in petty breaks in discipline has been a mislaid whisk-brush at room-inspection time. And though his penance will be completed at sundown, he may not, before that hour, pass that gate in the high brick wall even for such an important event as the arrival of a June Ball divinity.

But she is going to him in his imprisonment! My middle-aged heart gives a romantic throb. Imprisonment indeed! That enclosure looks as festive as a lawn fete.

The pretty greens are flowered with innumerable girls in tender-toned, fluffy frocks—girls holding court from benches beneath the trees, girls standing in a half-circle of middies, or girl and middy twosing off toward the shining water beyond.

We find the attractive Ben in a considerable group of other restricted middies, just inside the gate; and quite unabashed he comes forward. We enter this paradise, he and Margarita a little in advance, for she is, again in the vernacular, his "special," his invitation having outrun all others—hence the gleam in the tall boy's eye in pronouncing the hero's predicament.

As we walk, my education advances. My two charming cavaliers teach me to talk Annapolis, and it proves indeed an interesting language.

To fail to pass an examination is to "hit the tree;" if you fall short in the winter test, it is "hitting the Christmas tree;" while a spring down fall is cheerily accounted a collision with the "Maypole."

When you fail you are a "bilger," and should your withdrawal from the Academy be suggested you are being "unsat." The men who acquire high marks are "savoirs," the men who pull through with a scrape become known to fame as "wooden men."

The very few cadets who take no part in the hops and other social events are branded "red Mikes." The girl who becomes very popular is a "queen," while the occasional few girls (the red-haired, frank cousin volunteered this, but was scowled at by the tall brown middy) who prove stupid are ungallantly but confidentially termed "bricks."

Escort duty is always called "dragging" (derivation unknown), and you "drag a queen (or a brick) to the hop." By the time we reach the boat-landing, I feel I may in the future listen to middy conversation with a fair amount of intelligence.

The water scene is entrancing. The sun shines brilliantly, there is a splendid freshness in the air and a still more splendid freshness about all the gay young life.

More maids and middies embark and disembark from rowboats of all sizes. Sailboats skim toward the broad bay, where, in the distance, massive as if rooted, stand the grim hulls of battleships.

A middy may take a maid as far as the lighthouse, I am told, and there seems to me a suggestion of tender sentiment in these naval youngsters taking the idols of their youthful hearts on the sea that is to be their home for so much of the future. Margarita and Ben look off dreamily.

"But how about lunch?" suggests red-haired cousin; and we come back to earth and to Carvel Hall.

A perfect maelstrom of middies in dress uniform eddies about the corridors of Carvel Hall before it is yet dark, waiting for their queens to descend to dinner and the dance. For though a June Ball is honored with an hour's extension in closing, it begins promptly at eight, as do all dances under this healthy regime.

Just as we finish dinner some cadets outside have started to sing, and we step out to listen. It is "Anchors Aweigh"—the favorite of all middies, written by a middy—their own special property. The spirit of the navy rings through the song, and something chokes me as it pulses on those fresh voices through the June night.

But the next moment the singers are swinging away toward the Academy and there floats back a choppy lilt with irreverent words:

      Everybody works but John Paul Jones,
        And he lies around all day.
      Nicely pickled in alcohol, etc. etc.

It is a night in ten thousand: starry and purple, with sudden little currents of sweet-smelling warmth.

"No 'Chaney's best' tonight," remarks the cousin middy, looking at the stars; and it is elucidated that in very bad weather a cadet is permitted to "drag" his "queen" to the hop in a carriage—ironic concession, since the only liveryman in town is one "Chaney,"

[1897]

A mortar and Confederate guns, a favorite spooning spot [c. 1893]

whose stock consists of four or five dilapidated hacks—"Chaney's best."

Unless a middy turn highwayman and literally hold up one of these prehistoric four-wheelers, the chances are that he and his "queen" will not arrive until the dance is half over.

An Annapolis hop is the same delightful spectacle that all ballrooms full of dancers present: harmony of movement matched with harmony of music. But it is something besides. Even chaperons on the side lines feel it.

Beneath the fairyland scene lies the throb of patriotism. Those gay middies are to be Uncle Sam's defenders; the upholders of the nation's honor and pride before all other nations.

Taught to dance; taught to be charming in manner; taught to be disciplined and brave—no wonder a girl is at her best with from three to five of these cavaliers literally dancing attendance upon her!

There's no place for a wallflower to grow. At Annapolis every girl simply has to feel herself a queen. Future invitations will reveal whether or not she has really achieved that preeminence; but while she is there she is made to feel that it is true for at least once in her life.

Eight bells sounds, and the strange mixture of frivolity and discipline is again apparent, for on the first stroke music and dancing cease.

Every middy draws himself erect, all move forward toward the colors, hung aloft. And there this mass of pretty girls and wedge-shaped middies stand at "attention," facing the colors, while the band plays ever so beautifully, "The Star Spangled Banner." The June Ball is over.

There will come moments, I am sure, in the life of each of these girls, when she will remember those days when she was an Annapolis belle.

She will look back at them through rose-tinted glasses, and she will recollect only the sunshine of that stretch of greensward, the unruffled waters of the Severn and the dancing waves of the bay, the ballroom with its flags and scarlet-coated band and the perfect rhythm of her partners' step—uniforms and eager faces everywhere!

She will look back and rejoice that she was one of those selected from the thousands and thousands of her kind in America to come for a little time among the delights of this town where every girl is a belle.

Katherine G. Busbey

[1900–1902]

ORDER PROMULGATED

Brigade of Midshipmen Given Their Anti—Marriage Notice

Girls in search of husbands need not come to the Naval Academy, especially if they are bordering on the old-maid list, as hereafter and henceforth no brass-buttoned middy can wed until he is a full-fledged gold-laced officer with a commission in his vest pocket, if he wears a vest.

The order of the Secretary of the Navy forbidding midshipmen to marry until they have completed the required two years' cruise at sea was received at the Naval Academy yesterday and promulgated before the brigade. It is fully realized here that the sole ground of the department's ruling was because the middies cannot comfortably support a wife on the comparative small salary they receive unless they have other means.

It has been published that the order would probably hold up the wedding of Midshipman Hugh R. Van De Boe, of the present graduating class, but such is not the case. Mr. Van De Boe arranged nearly a fortnight ago with the Navy Department for the permission to be married on June 5. The new order is generally approved in naval circles.

Mr. Van De Boe stated to the Secretary that he wished to marry Miss Scott, daughter of Mrs. R. C. Scott, of Annapolis. He satisfied Secretary Meyer that he had sufficient independent means to maintain a wife, aside from his salary. His father is a wealthy real estate dealer of Cleveland, O. His family are now here for the wedding, which takes place Saturday, the day after Midshipman Van De Boe's graduation.

3 June 1909

MIDSHIPMEN GET NEW RANK SOON

First Annapolis Class to Receive Ensigns' Commissions Directly Upon Graduation.

MANY VERSATILE 'STARS'

[SPECIAL DESPATCH TO THE HERALD.]

ANNAPOLIS, Md., Saturday.—The one hundred and sixty-three members of the class of 1912 at the Naval Academy are feeling highly elated over the fact that they will be the first midshipmen ever graduated with the rank of ensign in the navy. Heretofore the diploma of graduation at Annapolis did not mean a commission in the service, as it does at West Point, but merely that a preparatory course had been completed and that two arduous years were before the graduate, years during which the work and responsibilities of officers were to be placed upon the young men, but without the pay, rank and privileges. Then came another set of severe examinations.

The passage of the law permitting the graduation of midshipmen with the rank of ensigns was one of the two things in connection with the Naval Academy that everybody admitted should be done, and no one could understand why it was not earlier accomplished. The other was the appropriation for a suitable sepulchre for the body of John Paul Jones, the father of the American Navy, which has been entombed beneath the stairway at Bancroft Hall. Finally Congress has met both demands, and when the members of the class of 1912 receive their diplomas next June it will be in the form of an ensign's commission, while the construction of the crypt for John Paul Jones' body in the new chapel will be undertaken at once.

Judging by its record in discipline, scholarship, athletics and the various departments of activity at the Naval Academy, the present class is well worthy of the honor of being graduated with commissions.

1912

Unofficial graduation exercises [c. 1915]

Class portraits came into vogue at the Naval Academy during the Civil War. Humor occasionally prevailed, as with the class of 1891, *below*, but more often the group photographs were traditional and formal. The honor inherent in being members of the class of 1900 apparently was not lost on the midshipmen who traveled to West Point to take part in the unique historical record, *opposite*.

The class of 1891 and friends

The classes of 1900 of the Naval Academy and the Military Academy

The class of 1861

The fiftieth reunion of the class of 1865